Freedom Readers

PIONEER EDITION

By Fran Downey

CONTENTS

Freedom
Readers

PRINTS & PHOTOGRAPHS DIVISION, LIBRARY OF CONGRESS

~~~~~~~~~ ◆◆◆ ~~~~~~~~~

What does reading mean to you? For African-American slaves, it meant freedom.

~~~~~~~~~ ◆◆◆ ~~~~~~~~~

By Fran Downey

You can read when you want to. That has not always been true. Long ago, most slaves could not read.

Owners were afraid to teach slaves to read. They feared that slaves who could read would want freedom.

The owners were right about that. Reading helped some slaves gain freedom. Let us meet a few of these freedom readers.

A Chief's Son
Olaudah Equiano

◆ ◆ ◆

Olaudah Equiano was born in Africa in 1745. Strangers **kidnapped** him when he was 10. They took him away. They sold him as a slave.

A sailor bought Equiano. He took him onto a ship. Then he forced the slave to work for him.

The slave saw his **master** reading books. He knew his master learned from books. But how?

The slave tried talking to the books. That did not work. He held books to his ears. They did not speak. Later, friends taught him to read.

Equiano grew up. He saved some money. He paid for his freedom. Then he moved to England.

There, he wrote his life story. His book asked people to end slavery.

Olaudah Equiano

Freedom Lost. *An American slave ship sails off the coast of Africa.*

The Poet
Phillis Wheatley

◆ ◆ ◆

Slave Sale. *Men, women, and children were sold at auctions like the one pictured.*

Phillis Wheatley

Phillis Wheatley was born in Africa. She was born in about 1753. Later, kidnappers caught her. They took her to America.

There, she was sold as a slave. John Wheatley bought her. She was 7.

The Wheatley family soon saw how smart she was. One of the children taught her to read and write.

At 13, Wheatley wrote her first poem. She wrote many more. Later, her poems were printed in a book. She was the first African-American woman to write a book.

Wheatley wrote many poems about freedom. She even met George Washington. She also wrote that slavery should end.

Freedom Fighter
Frederick Douglass

◆ ◆ ◆

Free at Last. *An artist shows President Abraham Lincoln meeting Frederick Douglass.*

Frederick Douglass

Frederick Douglass was born in about 1818. He grew up as a slave in Maryland.

At 10, Douglass wanted to read. His master's wife said she would teach him. He quickly learned the alphabet. He wanted to know more.

Then his master heard what was going on. He said slaves should not read. He stopped the lessons.

Douglass did not give up. He got other children to teach him to read. He also learned to write. Later, Douglass ran away.

He moved to the North. Slavery was **illegal,** or against the law, there.

Douglass became famous. He fought slavery. He made speeches. He wrote books. He ran a newspaper. His hard work helped end slavery.

More Freedom Readers

✦ ✦ ✦

Many other slaves also learned to read. No one knows how many. Reading could get a slave in trouble. So many slaves did not talk about it.

Lucius Holsey owned two spelling books. He learned all the words in the books.

Thomas Jones paid a child six cents a week to teach him to spell. The child taught him simple words. They had one or two **syllables,** or parts.

Sometimes slaves helped other slaves learn. That happened to Sella Martin. His friends knew he wanted to read. They helped him.

His friends stole books. They gave the books to Martin. The books helped him learn to read.

Slavery ended in 1865. Then many former slaves went to school. They knew they needed to learn to read. Reading would help them live as free people.

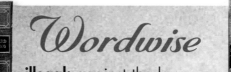

Wordwise

illegal: against the law

kidnap: to steal a person

master: slave owner

syllable: part of a word

On the Run. *Some slaves fled to the North in search of freedom.*

From Slavery

Hard Work. *Many freed slaves still worked on other people's farms. They did not have land of their own.*

to Freedom

Slaves were not allowed to read. They could not own land. They were not allowed to vote. They could not even get married.

Laws said slaves belonged to masters. Slaves had no rights. They were workers. That was all.

Farm Work

That changed in 1865. Nearly four million slaves were freed. For the first time, they had choices. Yet many stayed where they were. Some still farmed for their old masters. Why?

Freed slaves had few options. They had no education. They had little money to buy land or homes. True freedom was still a long way off.

Finding Freedom

Reading and writing were steps to freedom. These skills could help freed slaves get better jobs.

Some freed slaves went to school. They studied hard. They took no vacations. They just wanted to learn. Others learned to read in churches. Some were taught by friends who knew how to read.

Power to the People

Change did not happen overnight. But in time, freed slaves got other rights. They became citizens in 1868. They began to vote in 1870.

Freed slaves got more power. A few even served in Congress. They helped make the country stronger. But the changes were not nearly enough.

Attending School. *For African Americans, getting an education was one way to become truly free.*

The Costs of Freedom

Freed slaves still had problems. Many could not get an education. There were not enough schools.

Land and money were problems too. Freed slaves did not have enough money to buy land. They had to rent it from whites. They also had to pay for clothes and food. There was little money left over.

Free But Not Equal

Slaves got their freedom in 1865. But they faced many hardships. Some people still treated them like slaves. African Americans were free, but not yet equal.

They fought hard to be treated like other Americans. It took 100 years. But in the 1960s, they finally won equal rights.

Growing Problems. *Farming was expensive. Former slaves had to pay for land, animals, seeds, and tools.*

Finding Freedom

Read on to see what you learned about slavery and freedom.

1 Why did slaves want to read?

2 Who was Frederick Douglass? Why is he famous?

3 How did slaves learn to read?

4 What rights did slaves get after they were freed?

5 Why was life still hard for freed slaves?